William Edward Baxter

England and Russia in Asia

William Edward Baxter

England and Russia in Asia

ISBN/EAN: 9783744755610

Printed in Europe, USA, Canada, Australia, Japan

Cover: Foto ©ninafisch / pixelio.de

More available books at **www.hansebooks.com**

The Imperial Parliament

EDITED BY

SYDNEY BUXTON, M.P.

> In every free country it is of the utmost importance that all opinions extensively entertained, all sentiments widely diffused, should be *stated* publicly before the nation."—BAGEHOT.

ENGLAND AND RUSSIA.

ENGLAND AND RUSSIA IN ASIA.

BY THE RT. HON.
W. E. BAXTER, M.P.

Stereotyped  *Edition.*

London

SWAN SONNENSCHEIN & CO.,
PATERNOSTER SQUARE.

WORKS BY MR. SYDNEY BUXTON.

—:o:—

Two Volumes. 8vo. Price 26s.

FINANCE AND POLITICS: AN HISTORICAL STUDY, 1783—1885.

"A couple of extremely interesting and readable volumes."—*Spectator.*

"The value of these two volumes lies in their lucid exposition of the development of the true principles of taxation; but their interest not a little depends on their style, which is throughout vigorous and terse."—*Daily Telegraph.*

"Mr. Buxton . . . makes a sort of half-apology for the length to which his work has run out. He may, however, be certain that in the opinion of his readers no such excuse is needed. A title in which the word 'finance' occurs is, of course, a danger-signal for many people, showing them what to avoid by reason of its want of interest. In Mr. Sydney Buxton's case the warning would be false. He is always interesting."—*Scotsman.*

"A well-digested history of the government of England during the last hundred years . . . though the book must have been terribly hard to write, it is pleasantly easy to read. Mr. Buxton has the great gift of lucid statement; indispensable in dealing with those complicated questions of policy which have a special attraction for him."—*Liverpool Post.*

Seventh Edition, *enlarged, re-written, and with new subjects.*
Price 8s.

A HANDBOOK TO POLITICAL QUESTIONS,

WITH THE ARGUMENT ON EITHER SIDE.

"In times when almost every adult is a politician, such a publication as this Handbook ought to receive a widespread and hearty welcome. . . . The Handbook will be of service not only to general readers who have no time to follow every long debate in Parliament, but will also be appreciated by members of debating societies who wish to post themselves up in the leading points for and against modern proposals for reform in home policy."—*Leeds Mercury.*

JOHN MURRAY, ALBEMARLE STREET.

Third Edition. Ninth Thousand. Price 6d.

A POLITICAL MANUAL.

ALEXANDER AND SHEPHEARD, 27, CHANCERY LANE.

8vo. Price 3s. 6d.

A HANDBOOK TO THE DEATH DUTIES,

BY SYDNEY BUXTON, M.P. & GEORGE STAPYLTON BARNES, Barrister-at-Law.

"This is an admirably clear exposition of a very complicated subject. The history, the anomalies, and the reform of the Death Duties are successfully treated, in a manner so lucid and even so lively that he who runs may read. . . . Altogether it is one of the best political handbooks that we have lately come across."—*Pall Mall Gazette.*

"An interesting and valuable work, which may be regarded as the best text book on the subject."—*Speaker.*

"The book is a model of lucid explanation and masterly analysis."—*Manchester Examiner.*

JOHN MURRAY, ALBEMARLE STREET.

In Uniform Crown 8vo Volumes.
Price Ninepence.   Cloth One Shilling

The Imperial Parliament
Series.
Edited by SYDNEY BUXTON, M.P.
(Author of "Finance and Politics," "Handbook to Political Questions," etc.)

THE intention of this Series is to place within reach of the general public, at a very cheap rate, short volumes dealing with those topics of the day which lie within the range of practical politics.

Notwithstanding the constantly increasing demand for political literature, to enable electors and others to follow the argument in connection with particular reforms, there are no easily obtainable and permanent text-books to which they can refer, the advocates of these reforms confining themselves, as a rule, to pamphlets, magazine articles, and speeches, or else discussing their subjects in a form beyond the reach of the masses.

It is hoped that these little volumes, being written in a judicial spirit—and, though advocating each its own proposal, as far as possible, free from party bias or polemical controversy may be recognised as authoritative, and, being published in a permanent form, may be less evanescent than ordinary political writings, and be thus of real value. The Series, though "political," is not "Party."

The volumes are written by politicians who are recognized as authorities on the subjects of which they treat. Each volume is complete in itself, and the writers alone are responsible for the opinions they may express.

The Series comes into competition with no existing publication. The valuable "English Citizen" Series details the rights and responsibilities of citizens as they exist at present; it speaks of things as they are—this Series deals with them as reformers

The Following Volumes are Already Issued:

1. **IMPERIAL FEDERATION.** By the MARQUIS OF LORNE.
2. **REPRESENTATION.** By Sir JOHN LUBBOCK, Bart, M.P.
3. **LOCAL ADMINISTRATION.** By WILLIAM RATHBONE, M.P., ALBERT PELL, and F. C. MONTAGUE, M.A.
4. **ENGLAND AND RUSSIA IN ASIA.** By Right Hon. W. E. BAXTER.
5. **WOMEN SUFFRAGE.** By Mrs. ASHTON DILKE and WILLIAM WOODALL, M.P.
6. **LOCAL OPTION.** By W. S. CAINE, M.P., WILLIAM HOYLE, and Rev. DAWSON BURNS, D.D.
7. **LEASEHOLD ENFRANCHISEMENT.** By H. BROADHURST, M.P., and R. T. REID, M.P.
8. **DISESTABLISHMENT.** By the late H. RICHARD, M.P., and J. CARVELL WILLIAMS.
9. **REFORM OF LONDON GOVERNMENT AND OF CITY GUILDS.** By the late J. F. B. FIRTH, M.P.
10. **CHURCH REFORM.** By ALBERT GREY, CANON FREMANTLE, and others.

The Following Volumes are in Preparation:—

LAND REFORM. By the Right Hon. G. J. SHAW-FEFEVRE, M.P.

REFORM OF THE HOUSE OF LORDS. By JAMES BRYCE, M.P.

Other Volumes will follow, 1/- each Volume.

SWAN SONNENSCHEIN & CO.,
PATERNOSTER SQUARE.

If you Require Really Good Quality

Tea, Coffee, and General Groceries,

WRITE FOR

PRICE LIST AND SAMPLES,

WHICH WILL BE SENT FREE BY

PHILLIPS & CO.,

8, King William Street, or

THE SUPPLY STORES,

80 & 82, Clerkenwell Road.

Medals have been Awarded to this good, old-established Firm, for Purity of their Teas, etc.

Phillips & Co.'s Chocolates are Delicious.

CONTENTS.

CHAP.		PAGE
I.	INTRODUCTORY—THE "NATURAL ENEMY" DOCTRINE—STANDING ARMIES—A WAR BETWEEN ENGLAND AND RUSSIA ABOUT CENTRAL ASIA UNJUSTIFIABLE	11
II.	THE INTERNAL CONDITION OF RUSSIA AND HER WARS OF ANNEXATION—PROBABILITY OF A REVOLUTION	16
III.	RUSSIA A CIVILIZING POWER IN CENTRAL ASIA	20
IV.	ENGLAND AND RUSSIA HAVE THEIR RESPECTIVE MISSIONS IN CENTRAL ASIA—RUSSIAN DESIGNS ON INDIA RIDICULOUS—ANNEXATIONS OF THE TWO POWERS	31
V.	NECESSITY OF FIXING A NATURAL AND ENDURING BOUNDARY BETWEEN RUSSIA AND ENGLAND IN ASIA	43
VI.	THE CLOSE ALLIANCE WITH THE AMEER DANGEROUS—THE PROPOSED FRONTIER A MERE MAKESHIFT	48
VII.	CONCLUSION OF THE WHOLE MATTER	53

CONTENTS.

CHAP.		PAGE
VIII.	THE BEARING OF THE FOREGOING ON THE FEELING AND THE FINANCES OF INDIA—A PROVISO AND A CAUTION	55
IX.	THE RESPONSIBILITY OF WAR—BRITISH PUGNACITY—THE STANDING ARMIES OF EUROPE A MENACE AND DANGER—ARBITRATION A BETTER WAY	64

APPENDICES. 75
  1. "Macmillan's Magazine," June, 1885 . . 77
  2. Lord Ellenborough, October, 1842 . 84
  3. Sir John Lawrence, January, 1854 . . 85
       „   „   „   1857 . . 85
  4. Sir Richard Temple „ 1880 . 87
  5. Mackenzie's "Nineteenth Century" . . 88
  6. "Westminster Review," 1867 . . . 89
       „   „   1885 . . 89
  7. Sir H. R. Green, 1885 91
  8. "The Statesman's Year Book," 1885 . . 96

ENGLAND AND RUSSIA.

CHAPTER I.

INTRODUCTORY — THE "NATURAL ENEMY" DOCTRINE—
STANDING ARMIES—A WAR BETWEEN ENGLAND AND
RUSSIA ABOUT CENTRAL ASIA UNJUSTIFIABLE.

THE British people have been taught to believe that it is necessary for them to have a natural enemy, that they must always look on one or other of the great Powers with distrust and suspicion, and be prepared at any moment to engage with it in a sanguinary war. For generations France was the bugbear, and every schoolboy knows that we spent untold treasures and sacrificed thousands of brave men, in vain and futile endeavours to dictate in the governmental arrangments of that country, and to uphold in Europe a curious phantom called the "balance of power." Circumstances of late years have brought about a different state of feeling with respect to our neighbours on the other side of the Channel, and consequently alarmists, advocates of great military establishments, and people who think occasional wars not only unavoidable, but in some respects rather desirable, have been casting around for a foe to take the place of France.

When the civil war in the United States came to an end, they pointed to the fact that there were then 1,100,000 men under arms who were certain to invade Canada, to annex Jamaica, and to pay off old scores by subjecting us to every kind of national humiliation. The tone of a large portion of our press at that time amazed and amused the Americans, and the military element in this little pugnacious island seemed astonished, and rather disappointed, when a million of these dreaded troops returned at once to civil employments. For a time they looked in vain for "a foeman worthy of their steel," but the consolidation of Germany, and the remarkable display of its warlike might, encouraged new dreams, if not hopes. What could our little army do against these vast Teutonic hosts, disciplined as never men were before, educated in the science of war to an extent hitherto unknown, and flushed with victory over troops that had considered themselves invincible? From the old quarters sounded out anew the cry of danger, and it was only when the Germans laughed at us, just as the Americans had done, that newspaper editors and army officials found out that that cock would not fight either.

They fell back on Russia as a last resource. Rightly or wrongly, Englishmen had never forgiven the partition of Poland, and the lamentable events of the Crimean war have largely contributed to keep up the

INTRODUCTORY.

animosity; changes, too, were occurring in Central Asia which gave the war party in both countries opportunities of fanning the hostile feeling and strengthening the demand for increased armaments.

Both in London and St. Petersburg there are men of ability and rank and social importance, who do not despise efforts, of all kinds and in every direction, to persuade their fellow countrymen that a devastating war is inevitable, and that, with or without reason, the world must be convulsed by a struggle regarding the frontier question in Central Asia. It seems time, therefore, that some effort should be made on the part of those who do not believe in this doctrine of necessary war, who think these attempts to stir up bad blood discreditable and even criminal, to lay before the electors of this United Kingdom a plain statement, showing the facts of the case before they suffer themselves to be misled by men of war.

One cannot help feeling, in passing, that the maintenance of vast standing armies has a great deal to do with panics and unjust campaigns. The men, but more especially the officers, get tired of hum-drum drill and barrack life, and the mere pomp and pageantry of their profession; they long for a little excitement, for promotion, for higher pay, and the pickings of captured cities; and Europe is every now and then agitated by rumours of misunderstandings and probable conflicts, which have their origin

simply and solely in the natural desire of these idle and unproductive hosts to find employment. Napoleon the First called us a nation of shopkeepers; the truth is that we are the most pugnacious people on the face of the earth, credulous to a degree when told that our neighbours have designs upon us, and ready to fight in any part of the world, without taking the trouble to inquire whether or not we have justice on our side.

The purpose of the following pages is to show that the idea of going to war with Russia about Central Asia is wholly unjustifiable, and that there is no reason whatever why the two great nations should not come to a complete understanding which shall last, at all events, during this generation, and be of permanent benefit to countries which wild tribes and robber bands have hitherto kept in a state of perpetual turmoil.

No devoted admirer of the heavenly sentiment, "on earth peace and good-will toward men," can have observed, without anxiety and alarm, the tendency to magnify the importance of paltry territorial disputes, and so to light both in Europe and Asia the torch of war.

Any one venturing to write upon such a subject as this ought, of course, to have read most of, if not all, the literature relating to it, and to have studied every book on Russia that has been published for some years past, from the fierce and graphic attacks of Stepniak, to the two de-

lightful books of travel published by Dr. Lansdell. Unfortunately, both writers in the press and political orators have been inflaming the passions of their fellow-countrymen, without having taken the trouble to make themselves acquainted with what has been really going on in Central Asia, and with a very slight ethnographical and geographical knowledge of the question.

Liberals and Conservatives, alike, have recently more than ever taken up the question of financial reform and retrenchment of expenditure; but really it seems a sort of mockery to expatiate upon a million or two more or less on the face of the estimates, while a sore is being kept open that may at any moment add a hundred millions to the National Debt. It is useless to expect any substantial diminution of our burdens, any large remission of taxation, unless our foreign policy be placed on a sound and peaceful basis; our expenditure depends, not exclusively, but in a great measure, on our foreign policy, and any possible decrease we may effect in the cost of the Civil Service will always be but a flea-bite in comparison with the amount which may be at any moment added to the army and navy expenditure by a meddling, bullying, "Rule, Britannia" tone, assumed by our Government towards other nations. Over and over again Mr. Fox expounded this great truth to an ignorant, indolent, and heedless House of Commons.

CHAPTER II.

THE INTERNAL CONDITION OF RUSSIA AND HER WARS OF ANNEXATION—PROBABILITY OF A REVOLUTION.

It may be well to premise by saying, that the general belief held by those who deprecate a foolish jealousy of Russia, and unreasoning suspicion of her designs, is by no means one of approbation of her present government, or confidence in her future prosperity. They are for the most part pronounced Liberals, who abhor despotism, and who do not for a moment think that what the late Sir David Wedderburn, as reported in his most interesting Life by his sister, called "that honey-combed Colossus," can much longer exist without a revolution, which will show its inherent weakness, and the false and rotten foundation on which rests the edifice of its too-extended empire.

"I cannot help thinking," says Mr. Edward Rae, "that we shall one day see a break-up in the system of Russian social and religious existence, and the cataclysm when it does come will be a frightful one."

In corroboration of this opinion, it may be useful to

CONDITION OF RUSSIA. 17

give a few sentences from Stepniak's last work, "Russia under the Tzars":

"Russia is passing through a crisis of great importance in her social and political life. Within a brief space of time the revolutionary movement has attained a marvellous growth, and is spreading more and more among the classes which have heretofore been the chief supporters of the established order. . . . Discontent with the present *régime* has deepened and spread among all classes. It is no longer the army, but the flower of the Russian people that is rising against despotism; it is no longer an isolated attack, but an implacable war, without truce or intermission, between the Russian nation and its government. The fortress is crowded with prisoners. During the last twenty years hundreds have passed through it, and are being followed by more hundreds without pause or let. . . . In one way or another the catastrophe must come. There are observers who find many points of likeness between modern Russia and France before the Revolution. There is a good deal of analogy indeed, the greatest being, as touching Russia, the diffusion throughout all classes of the nation of anti-governmental tendencies, and of those generous and creative ideas which are called 'subversive' because they tend to subvert wrong and institute right."

The more one considers the condition of Russia—her impaired credit, the grinding taxation of her people, the universal dishonesty of her officials, the financial burdens imposed by the newly annexed provinces, the terrible conscription, the great loss caused to the nation by the innumerable fast-days, the huge mistake committed in neglecting commercial considerations when making the railroads, in consequence of which America and other countries have nearly ruined her corn trade—the more one feels the force of Mr. Gallenga's summing-up:

"All engrossed with her ambitious schemes of territorial aggrandizement, and only anxious about the development of her land and sea forces, Russia has suffered her trading institutions to lag behind those of the most primitive nations; and it seems difficult to foresee, in the sad state of the Imperial Treasury and the shattered condition of so many private fortunes, how she may be capable of such strenuous exertions as would enable her to make up for lost time."

One might go on heaping proof upon proof of the rotten state of Russia, and of the imminent probability of a catastrophe which will sweep away the autocracy, and show the real nature of that nightmare which disturbs the rest of timorous Britons. The conquests of the Czar, actual and imaginary, can have no other effect than to hasten the bitter end.

"I regard the immense extent of Russia as a real danger," said the Emperor Nicholas to Sir Hamilton Seymour in 18—; and he added, "If an Emperor of Russia should one day chance to conquer Constantinople, or should find himself forced to occupy it permanently, from that day would date the decline of Russia." It is perfectly clear, that if Russia were to extend her dominions in the direction of the Mediterranean or the Indian Ocean, "the entire equilibrium of the government," to use the words of Mr. Augustus Hare, "would be destroyed."

CHAPTER III.

RUSSIA A CIVILIZING POWER IN CENTRAL ASIA.

THE next point that requires the consideration of thoughtful people, is whether the influence of Russia in Central Asia is beneficial or the reverse; whether, with all her numerous defects, she is not acting as a civilizing agent in vast territories hitherto given up to lawlessness, to robber-bands, and to slavery and the slave-trade in their most cruel forms.

Let us put the inquiry in the words of Elihu Burritt: "There is Russia deploying southward on her march across the continent. Is she not the only power on earth in position to do the work of Christian civilization for the northern half of Asia?"

That is the view of one of the most shrewd of American writers.

An Englishman, Mr. Hepworth Dixon, expresses himself as follows: "The Russian will push his way until Khiva and Bokhara fall into his power. Why should we English regret his march, repine at his success? Is he not fighting for all the world a battle of law and order

and of civilization? Would not Russia at Bokhara mean the English at Bokhara also? Would not roads be made and stations built and passes guarded through the Steppe for traders and travellers of every race?" and Mr. Mackenzie, a Scotchman, in his invaluable book, "The Nineteenth Century," takes exactly the same view:

"Russia has subjugated innumerable wandering tribes to whom law and order were unknown. She has not bestowed on them a high civilization—for they were not able to receive it, and she herself does not possess it; but to the extent of their capacity she is teaching them to be orderly and industrious. Wherever her arms have been carried, slavery has been abolished. Her teaching is always stern, often cruel. It is not in her nature to impart, nor in that of her subjects to receive, any other. Her influence has, however, beyond doubt, been beneficial to those who have been brought under its sway."

In fact, it would be difficult indeed to find any author of a contrary opinion, but as this is a question of evidence, and one of the deepest importance to humanity, no apology need be offered for quoting the testimony of recent travellers. Their statements are the result of personal observation, for the most part were written on the spot, and, being as yet uncontradicted, should go far to remove the prejudices of the British public.

In his "Land Journey from Asia to Europe," Mr.

Whyte says: "Russian influence, there can be little doubt to an observing mind, will gradually absorb the whole of Mongolia, and it will be a very good thing too."

The following is from Mr. Douglas Freshfield's "Travels in the Central Caucasus": "We found, invariably, that in proportion as the natives are brought into contact with their rulers, they improve in manners and civilization, and that the districts which the Russians have left to take care of themselves are those in which the old customs of petty warfare, robbery and murder still prevail."

Hear Mr. MacGahan in his "Campaigning on the Oxus": "I believe that with the progress of the Russians in Central Asia, the whole country between the Syr and the Amu will one day blossom as the rose"

Here is the testimony of Major Wood, "Shores of Lake Aral": "And if a strong government which preserves social order, and has put down brigandage, slavery, and man-stealing, is worthy of sympathy, it is impossible not to feel that in undertaking the thankless and costly task of introducing civilization into Turkestan, Russia is fully entitled to the good wishes and gratitude of every Christian nation. . . . Those who often deplore the low type of the civilization which Russia introduces into Central Asia may at least take comfort in the reflection that every-

thing is for the best in this best of all worlds, since she alone perhaps, among the Great European Powers, is capable, from the very simplicity of her social institutions, of conferring on these Asiatic Nomads the very benefits which as yet they are able to comprehend and can feel grateful for."

"The Russian movements in Central Asia," Mr. Eugene Schuyler writes in his book on Turkestan, "have been marked by great discipline and humanity."

Now we come to Dr. Lansdell's last work, "Russian Central Asia": "But besides the Russian peasants who have become colonists by choice, and the Cossacks, who are sometimes made her colonists without their choice, there is a third class of settlers in Semirechia— natives from the neighbouring countries—who, sensible of the greater security to life and property, as well as lighter taxation, choose to be under the government of the Tzar rather than that of their Asiatic rulers. . . . The increase of cultivation, and therefore of the well-being of the population in the Amu-Daria Province, is traced to the feeling of security inspired among the natives by the Russian administration protecting them from pillage, and distributing among them equality of taxation"—such conditions, says the report, "as always accompany Russian conquests in Central Asia. . . . We were now only 7,500 paces, or say five miles,

from Russian territory, where one may find the newest outcome of the intelligence of the nineteenth century, yet we seemed to have dropped from the clouds among men and things 3,000 or 4,000 years behind."

The British people glory in having been the main instruments in putting an end to the oceanic slave-trade, and in having used their moral influence all over the world against slavery in every form. Russia has been doing precisely the same thing in Central Asia.

Mr. MacGahan says: "The Persian and other slaves hailed with wild delight the approach of the Russians; for the emancipation of the slaves has always followed the occupation of any place in Central Asia by the Russians."

"O. K." in "Skobeleff and the Slavonic Cause," writes: "But it was done at last and thoroughly. There are no slaves in the Akhal oasis to-day; nor any slave-dealers to carry on the practice of man-stealing. Russia answers for order along the Persian border. It is the latest addition to the police duty of the world which Russia has undertaken for mankind."

On this subject Dr. Lansdell's remarks are valuable: "When Kaufmann's army was approaching Khiva in 1873, the Khan released 12 captives; but when the Russians entered the Khanate they repaid the gracious act of Nadir Shah, and released 15,000 Persians, or, as

MacGahan says, 27,000, and Réclus 37,000. . . . On such occasions the Merv Tekkes take away as many men and women as suits them to keep or sell for slaves, and the rest they usually kill or sometimes maim by cutting off hands or feet."

Colonel Stewart says : "No one in England has any conception of the fearful sufferings of the slave-trade that has been carried on by the Turkomans." He believes that the number of slaves in Bokhara, Khiva, and Turkomania itself, a few years since, amounted to more than 100,000.

I observe that Baron Benoist-Mechin estimates, on what he considers good information, that within the last forty years "the Turkomans took away from Persia about 200,000 captives."

It may be said that these are *all* partial, and the last *too friendly*, witnesses. Then listen to Monsieur Vambéry, who certainly cannot be thus described :

"The abominable traffic in slaves, I am happy to remark, has, since the time of my sojourn in Bokhara, if not entirely ceased, yet certainly greatly abated; and it is very probable that ere long slaves will not be exposed for sale at all in Central Asia. For the cessation of this horrible practice we are indebted to Russia, who has forbidden the slave trade in her own Asiatic possessions, as well as in the countries under her protection. Nor

can the Turkomans, the chief man-stealers, continue as before their inroads into Persia to carry away men and cattle."

The good work of Russia in this part of the world has by no means yet been completed; nominally the slave markets in Bokhara have been closed, but Dr. Lansdell tells us that slaves are bought and sold with perfect freedom in all parts of the country, the Emir himself taking an active part in the traffic for the replenishment both of his harem and of his coffers, while robber bands infest the oases of Turkestan rendering travelling exceedingly dangerous. Dr. Lansdell sums up thus:

"After seeing Bokhara and Khiva under Asiatic rulers, and Tashkend and Samarkand under Europeans, I should be false to my convictions if I withheld my opinion that the natives have been gainers by the Russian conquest. Hence, now that Merv is annexed, if there are any that would rather see it revert to its old condition of lawlessness and slavery, and blood, I confess I am not one of the number."

Lord Edmond Fitzmaurice, M.P., who brings to bear upon the subject ample official knowledge and a most impartial mind, speaking in Glasgow only the other day, comes to the same conclusion. He said: "There was no question of foreign affairs upon which it was so neces-

sary to appeal to the reason and the common sense of one's fellow countrymen as upon this one of Central Asia, because there was an unfortunate tendency in this question always to place the worst construction upon whatever was done; and in that manner, he would not say to create difficulties, but to make difficulties where they existed larger and more formidable than they otherwise would be. He was not going to deny that the moment when the British soldier and the Russian soldier, when the Sepoy and the Cossack, found themselves in close proximity on Asiatic territory was not one of great anxiety, and that moment, if it had not actually come, was getting exceedingly near, when there was interposed between us only a kingdom like Afghanistan, which to a very great extent in its foreign relations was dependent upon us. It was therefore absolutely necessary to look the facts in the face. The manner to approach this question, and to avoid the dangers which otherwise we might fall into, was, in the first place, to make up our minds to do justice to every other Power, and not merely to claim it for ourselves. He had always contended that although the moment when the Sepoy and the Cossack came near one another would be one of difficulty and danger, nevertheless no person with a candid mind could possibly deny that in many respects the advance of Russia in Central Asia had been a gain to

civilization. Some of the fairest regions of the earth, or what were at one time the fairest regions of the earth, which had been devastated and turned into an absolute desert by the hordes of the man-stealing Turkomans, had by the Russian advance been restored to order and civilization. When the Russians took Khiva they were said to have liberated no fewer than 60,000 slaves, and the slavery which existed in that part of the world was, in the opinion of the few travellers who had succeeded at enormous risks in penetrating into those regions, one of the most horrible forms of slavery that ever existed in the world. Therefore he said it was our duty to realize the fact that this advance of Russia was not a matter in regard to which we ought to take the line of denying to Russia the same right to advance up to a certain point as we had claimed for ourselves in India. What was the great justification of our rule in India? What was the great justification of our original conquest of that country? It was this—that India had fallen into such a condition of anarchy that the life of man had become intolerable in it, and it had only been since the advance of British rule that peace and order had existed. In the same way the Russians might claim that their advance in Asia was rendered necessary owing to the fact that their neighbours were those barbarous and nomad hordes which in that part of the world also had

rendered life impossible to any except the robber and the marauder."

It has been lately the fashion, especially by that part of the British public called "Society"—who never were in the right, or on the winning side, on any foreign question in our time—to accuse Russia, in every successive advance of hers in Asia, of perfidy and bad faith. Not one in a hundred of them probably ever heard of Prince Gortchakoft's despatch, dated Nov. 21, 1864, in which he laid down principles that justify every single step that has been taken. It would be desirable that these false accusers should not only make themselves masters of this important document, but peruse with the care which it deserves the remarkably able and lucid speech delivered in the House of Lords by the Duke of Argyll, in May last. His trenchant criticism knocks from under their feet every foundation of Jingo attack, and thus does he dispose of the subject regarding which so much evidence has been produced in the foregoing pages :

" My lords, there is no denying that the tribes of the Khanates of Khiva and Bokhara are essentially robber tribes. If your lordships look at one of the works of Sir H. Rawlinson you will see that he mentions especially that one of the most fatal blows given to Khiva was that, by the subjugation of certain tribes outside the border, they lost a large revenue from the slave marts. I do not know

whether your lordships have observed in some communications from a correspondent of one of the London papers with Sir P. Lumsden's force, that he gives most distinct and emphatic testimony to the fact that the country until the Russian conquest had been wholly desolate, and he added that the Russians were not in Merv twelve months, when cultivation was rapidly extending wherever it was possible."

CHAPTER IV.

ENGLAND AND RUSSIA HAVE THEIR RESPECTIVE MIS-
SIONS IN CENTRAL ASIA—RUSSIAN DESIGNS ON INDIA
RIDICULOUS—ANNEXATIONS OF THE TWO POWERS.

IT is high time that the people of this country should realize the fact that Great Britain and Russia have their respective missions to perform in Asia quite independently of each other—to use the words of Colonel Maycosky to Dr. Lansdell, "as rivals, not as foes." So far from there being any necessary antagonism, those who look at the question in all its bearings, and from every point of view, will have no difficulty in coming to the same conclusion as the Rev. Malcolm MacColl, who, in his interesting book on the Eastern problem, says, "There are not two States in the world whose interests so imperatively demand mutual co-operation on the part of their respective Governments. Let it go forth throughout the East that there is an *entente cordiale* between Russia and England, and neither country need fear any rebellion on the part of its Asiatic subjects. It is in

our mutual hostility that the hopes of the disaffected lie."

Impartial foreigners have long ago come to this conclusion. It is many years since Elihu Burritt, the American, wrote: "The same suspicion has involved England in this wasteful and deplorable antagonism to Russia on the Eastern Question. This antagonism arrays her against the progress of Christian civilization and allies her to the most paralyzing despotism in the world. It belies and degrades the great position she claims as the van-leader of free nations and the institutions of freedom."

And more recently another distinguished American, Mr. Eugene Schuyler, thus expresses his opinion: "The attitude of England toward Russia with regard to Central Asia can hardly be called a dignified one. There are constant questions, protests, demands for explanations, and even threats—at least in the newspapers and in Parliament—but nothing ever is done. Outcries were made about the expedition to Khiva, but when the occupation had once become a *fait accompli* the same men and the same journals said that no harm was done. Again there were outcries and questions about the possibility of a Russian movement on Kashgar. Now after Khokand is occupied the conquest of Kashgar is looked upon as not so alarming after all. At present there is a similar uneasiness about Merv, and the

Russophobist party are using all their efforts to show, either that the Russians must not be allowed to take Merv, or if they do take it that Herat must be occupied. In all probability Merv will be occupied by the Russians, and in all probability the English Government will do nothing at all. It would seem wiser and more dignified, instead of subjecting the Russian Foreign Office to constant petty annoyances, to allow the Russians plainly to understand what limits they could not pass in their onward movement. A state of mutual suspicion bodes no good to the relations of any Governments."

In Germany the feeling is universal, the press bearing witness that our jealousy of, and interference with, Russia in Central Asia are quite indefensible; and Mr. Greene, in his "Sketches of Army Life in Russia," makes a statement not very complimentary to us as a nation, but unfortunately true: "England, on the other hand, has been the perpetual objector and obstructionist throughout the whole of this natural development of history, which however she has not succeeded in greatly retarding, though her action has engendered many hatreds and prolonged much misery."

Mr. Mackenzie Wallace, who has an intimate knowledge of Russia, tells us that "we ought to know Russia better and thereby avoid unnecessary collisions."

Part of this knowledge necessary to be acquired, is

that the mission of Russia is to annex and to introduce comparative civilization into regions in Asia quite out of our beat. A sentence from Colonel, now Sir Charles, McGregor's book, "Khorassan in 1875," remarkably illustrates this position: "The Tacmoorees all said that if the Kujjurs were not such contemptible characters, they would go and take them and release their people; they would one and all go and fight the Toorkmanns. But they could expect nothing from the Kujjurs, and they eagerly asked when the Russians were coming, adding, ' May God send them speedily!'"

But, say the men of war, you are altogether on the wrong scent; incidentally Russia may exercise a certain amount of civilizing influence over these wild tribes, but her real object is the conquest of India. Let us examine in a little detail this most gratuitous and almost ludicrous assumption, continually made and made without a shadow of proof, except the utterances of youthful Russian officers, some of whom are rather fond of poking fun at the arch enemy. The following extract from Mr. MacColl's work puts the question in the clearest possible light:

"Has Russia any designs on India? 'It is not at all to our interests,' says the memorandum of Russian policy, communicated to our Government

last June, 'to trouble England in her Indian possessions.' It is the settled belief of a large section of Englishmen that Russia is pursuing her conquests in Central Asia for the purpose of pushing her frontier to some convenient point from which she may be able to invade India. In considering the possibility of such an enterprise it is necessary to remember that the conditions of warfare have greatly changed since the Oriental expedition of Alexander the Great. An army now requires a very different train from that which would have sufficed for the days of spears and bows and arrows. The campaign which has just ended has lasted more than nine months reckoning from the crossing of the Turkish frontier to the signature of the armistice at Adrianople; and it has required the active service, from first to last, of at least 400,000 soldiers. Yet Turkey lies close to the enemy's frontier. No hostile population intervened, and no physical barriers of any moment had to be surmounted. We may safely assert, therefore, that a prudent commander would not undertake the conquest of India from any base of operation open to Russia with an army of less than 500,000. Half that number would probably be required to keep open his lines of communication. But let us suppose for argument's sake that an army of 200,000 would give Russia a bare chance of success.

That host with all its necessary equipments Russia would have to transport through hundreds of miles of what is, to a large extent, a trackless waste. Through most of it there are no other roads than camel paths. An army of the size I have supposed would therefore require, according to the estimate of military experts, a transport service of about 400,000 camels, 300,000 horses, and 1,500,000 camp followers. And what should we be doing in the meantime? We should be doing two things. We should be making preparations to meet the attack on a scale commensurate with the occasion and with our vast resources, and our agents would be busy stirring up disaffection in the rear of the invaders and hampering their communications over an extent of roadless territory so vast as to be incapable of being effectively guarded.

"Considering the difficulties and dangers Russia had to encounter in invading so puny a Power as Khiva, it is easy to estimate the risks she would have to face in a march to India. Financially the enterprise would be most ruinous. But let us postulate another miracle, and assume that the Russian army escaped all the perils and difficulties which I have indicated, and which in fact would be insurmountable. Let us suppose that it arrived 200,000 strong, and thoroughly equipped at the base of the lofty mountains which guard our

Indian Empire. The mouths of the passes are in our possession, besides a series of detached forts and military stations scattered along our frontier at the foot of the mountains. Here, supposing it to advance so far without molestation, the Russian army would find us fresh and ready to give it a warm reception—behind us boundless resources in men and money, plains seamed by railways, and an ocean owning our undisputed sway. Defeat to the Russian army under such circumstances would be absolute ruin. Its prestige gone, swarms of enemies would rise up behind and around it to cut off its retreat. And the blow of so great a disaster would reverberate far beyond the Indus; it would imperil not only the Asiatic position of Russia—it would shake her to her centre even in Europe. Let us, however, make another concession for the sake of argument. Let us suppose that our arms received a check in our first encounter with Russia. This, no doubt, would be a serious mishap, as it might encourage disaffection on the part of some of our native population. But we should have made ample preparation for such a contingency, and, with the certainty of being able to rely on the loyalty of our most warlike tribes in the emergency, we should be able to dispute the advance of Russia step by step, while at the same time harassing her in the rear. But if, contrary to all reasonable calculations, Russia should succeed in breaking our

power in India, and driving us to our ships, even in that case she would be only at the threshold of her difficulties. Having got rid of us she would have to begin afresh the conquest of India for herself. Her only chance against us would lie in the seduction of some of our Indian subjects from their allegiance; thus turning their arms against us. But it is safe to say that no appreciable section of the people of India would help Russia to break our yoke for the purpose of having her own imposed in its stead. If they assisted her to get rid of us at all it would certainly be in order to get rid of foreign rule altogether. So that Russia, after driving us out of the country, would find herself surrounded by hostile populations—both those who helped her against us and those who fought on our side—all eager to drive her after us. The defeat of the English rule in India therefore, supposing it possible, would be only the beginning of Russia's troubles. She would have to subdue India to her own rule and reorganize its Civil Service; and no one who will take the trouble to think out the problem can doubt that long before its solution India would accomplish the ruin of Russia. The task is one which, under such favourable conditions as Russia could not expect, has taken ourselves more than a century to fulfil. Thus we see that, when the theory of a Russian conquest of India is dragged out into the light and confronted with what the

late Emperor Napoleon used to call the 'irresistible logic of facts,' it is found to have no more substance in it than a nursery bogey.

"Lord Hardinge, who afterwards succeeded the Duke of Wellington as Commander-in-chief, characterized the fear of a Russian invasion of India as 'a political nightmare.' 'Lord Hardinge is quite right,' said the Duke, when this was reported to him. 'Rely upon it you have nothing to fear from Russia in that direction.'

"So much as to the possibility of Russia conquering India if she wished it. But does she wish it? She is a country which is supposed, even by those who fear and dislike her most, to understand her own interest uncommonly well. Would it, then, be to the interest or Russia to acquire India, even if she could do so without firing a shot or sacrificing a man? My belief is that, on the mere ground of an enlightened self-interest, Russia would decline the perilous gift of India if England were to make her the offer of it."

On a subject of this kind every one will agree that the opinion of General Skobeleff ought to be regarded with the utmost respect, and "O. K." tells us that he "was a great adherent of my favourite dream of an Anglo-Russian alliance. He greatly admired England. 'What a pity,' he said once to me, 'Russia and England know

so little of each other. In Asia they could co-operate and work together.' . . . As to a Russian invasion of India he said, 'I do not understand military men in England writing in *The Army and Navy Gazette*, which I read, of a Russian invasion of India. I should not like to be commander of such an expedition. The difficulties would be enormous. To subjugate Akhal we only had 5,000 men, and needed 20,000 camels. To get that transport we had to send to Orenburg, to Khiva, to Bokhara, and to Mangishlak for camels. The trouble was enormous. To invade India we should need 150,000 troops—60,000 to enter India with, and 90,000 to guard the communications. If 5,000 men needed 20,000 camels, what would 150,000 need? and where could we get the transport? We should require vast supplies, for Afghanistan is a poor country and could not feed 60,000 men; and we should have to fight the Afghans as well as you.' On my urging that the Afghans might be tempted by the bribe of the spoilation of India to side with the Russians, he said: 'I doubt it. To whom could we offer the bribe? If we bribed one Sirdar, you would bribe another. If we offered one rouble, you (England) would offer two; if we offered two you would offer five—you would beat us in that. No; the Afghans would fight us as readily as they fought you. . . . Do you know (here he rose and spoke with vehemence,

regarding me with a smile), I consider the Central Asia question all humbug.'"

No one doubts the absolute impartiality of Mr. Schuyler, or the opportunities he had of acquiring information, and here is his testimony, given at the close of his extensive wanderings: "It is impossible to believe that there is any settled intention on the part of the Russian Government of making an attack on India, or even of preparing the way for it; nor is there any desire for the possession of India."

Dr. Lansdell gives evidence precisely to the same effect: "It took six camels and two horses to run me and my carpet-bag across the Aralo-Caspian desert. What, then, would it take to move an army? Nor can I express an opinion as to whether the Russians have the least desire to attempt such a thing. No doubt there are Turkestan officers — to whom war means medals, promotion, and money—who are quite ready to attempt the invasion of India, or, for that matter, of Timbuctoo or any other place, as there are Indian officers who, for similar reasons, would invade Turkestan. But I was not led, by anything I saw or heard in Central Asia, to think that there was any preparation or desire for an invasion; and when now and then I broached the subject to Russian officers, it never elicited any suspicious remarks, or was treated otherwise than as a joke."

The war party in Great Britain is never tired of accusing Russia of the lust of conquest and undue territorial annexation. "People who live in glass-houses shouldn't throw stones." The following figures, from an instructive article contributed by Mr. Farrer to *The Fortnightly Review*, emphasize the truth of the proverb: "During the last 130 years England has conquered 2,650,000 square miles, and nearly 250,000,000 people. These figures do not include Australia, or any territory annexed without conquest. She has also established a garrison on every coign of vantage in every quarter of the globe. On the other hand, Russia has conquered, within the last 130 years, 1,642,000 square miles, but only 17,135,000 people—that is, about one-fifteenth of our conquered population during the same period."

CHAPTER V.

NECESSITY OF FIXING A NATURAL AND ENDURING BOUNDARY BETWEEN RUSSIA AND ENGLAND IN ASIA.

BRITISH and Russian statesmen cannot much longer delay to fix a boundary between their Asiatic possessions, which shall be natural, scientific, and likely to endure. England must unquestionably safeguard India by the adoption, after consulting the best military authorities, of a frontier line which shall, to all intents and purposes, be impregnable; and can then safely leave the Russians to roam over Central Asia at their own sweet will, with the certainty, that the further they roam, the worse it will be for them both politically and financially, and in the comfortable belief that China, not England, is the Power with which they will ultimately have to settle. Mr. Gallenga says:

"There remains the Asiatic side, where England finds, in a great measure, herself alone face to face with Russia. But there geography is England's ally. Between English and Russian Asia deserts, mountains, or seas

raise an almost insurmountable barrier—insurmountable, at least, till Russia multiply her locomotive means on land by hundreds or thousands, or till she become a first-rate maritime Power. With respect to roads, or railroads, they are as yet in Russia, and especially in Asiatic Russia—an institution in its infancy. And as to naval strength, that must be commensurate with a nation's mercantile marine, and in that respect the State that comes next to England is neither Russia nor France, but Germany. Notwithstanding the sad experience of the Crimea, and the more recent Turkish wars, it seems reasonable to believe that, whatever bitter messages diplomatists may be tempted to exchange, in whatever bluster and 'tall talk' statesmen or soldiers may love to indulge, and however matters may be carried, even to the extremity of drawn swords, the day for a real, serious, life-and-death quarrel between Russia and England is as yet remote; and until the absolute necessity for an appeal to arms arises, wherefore should there not be peace and forbearance from mutual provocation and gratuitous insult?"

Many of our wisest and ablest Indian administrators, both civil and military, regret that we ever crossed the Indus, and consider that river the natural boundary of our possessions in the North-west. In the fourth chapter of the second volume of Lord

Lawrence's Life there is an exceedingly interesting argument upon this question, which will amply repay perusal. The following sentences contain the gist of it:
"The Chief Commissioner is strongly inclined to the opinion that the best policy would be to confine ourselves to the line of the Indus in that quarter. The Chief Commissioner has arrived at this conclusion after careful consideration and much reluctance. His views were all the other way. It has only been by slow degrees and long consideration that he has formed this opinion. The line of the Indus possesses the following advantages over that of the mountain range. It is considerably shorter, and therefore requires fewer troops for its defence. The river is in itself a mighty bulwark, broad, deep, and rapid. It has no fords. Maharaja Runjeet Sing once, indeed, crossed his cavalry near Jorbella into Eusufzaie, but he lost five hundred horsemen in so doing. An able engineer, at a moderate cost, would make the left bank of the Indus impregnable against an invader. . . . The districts beyond the Indus cost us, under the best arrangements, at least fourfold their income. This money, otherwise expended, would add to our material resources greatly. We really neither conciliate the people nor the Afghan nation. If the friendship of the Afghans is to be gained, if it is indeed worth having, this object is more likely to be

accomplished by surrendering these important possessions, which to them would prove invaluable, but to us would ever continue a fruitful source of danger, expense, and loss of life."

The great river, however, has been crossed, and we must make the best of the situation. Lord Lawrence's biographer says : "The boundaries of the Punjab and of India are clearly marked out by the hand of Nature. On the north the Himalayas give it an absolute security from Chinese or Tartar, or even Russian scares, while on the west the range of the Suliman Mountains, which runs parallel with the Indus, forms an almost equally impenetrable barrier. It is true, indeed, that the Suliman range is traversed by passes, which under favourable circumstances have given an entrance to the invading armies of Alexander the Great and Timour the Tartar, of Badir and Nadir Shah. But those conquerors were opposed by no foe worthy of the name. And, happily for us, here again range upon range rises behind the main mountain wall, and beyond these once more are 'wilds immeasurably spread,' which, being inhabited by races as rough, as wild, and as inhospitable as the soil on which they dwell, altogether form an all but impregnable protection to India. No better series of defences, indeed, scientific or natural, could possibly be desired against any foe who comes from beyond Afghan-

istan; and no strong foe, it should be remarked, can ever come from within it."

Surely it becomes our duty, as it clearly is our interest, to apply the resources of modern science to this mighty natural wall, so as to render it a sure defence, and put an end to these continual panics and alarms, which are a reflection on our statesmanship and a disgrace to our common Christianity.

CHAPTER VI.

THE CLOSE ALLIANCE WITH THE AMEER DANGEROUS—
THE PROPOSED FRONTIER A MERE MAKESHIFT.

THOUGHTFUL people are rapidly coming to the conclusion that this intimate alliance with the Ameer is nearly as great a blunder as the late utterly indefensible war with his predecessor. The fickleness of the Afghan race has become a proverb in the East, and as soon as their rulers think that our presents and subsidies are likely to come to an end, they may throw themselves into the arms of Russia. Are we prepared to guarantee their good faith, and their respect for the frontier — a makeshift and temporary frontier—which is now being mapped out? Would it not be far better to look the question fairly in the face, to consider our dominions practically conterminous with those of Russia, and to arrange a boundary which shall not be dependent upon the doings of wild Turkoman tribes, or unsettled, shifty, and semi-barbarous governments at Cabul?

On this subject, it is both interesting and instructive to watch the opinion prevalent among other nations.

In Germany there seems, indeed, to be no two opinions in the matter. The enlightened public there have long realized the fact that it is against our interest to interfere in Central Asia, and that the present negotiations are founded on a wrong basis, as being far too dependent upon the life of an Asiatic potentate, and the caprice of a fickle people. They especially consider us as being in a false position in regard to Herat, the inhabitants of which detest the Afghans proper and the supporters of Abdurrahman, and are admittedly ready at any moment to welcome the Russians. "Never did people," says Monsieur Vambéry—and his testimony cannot be disputed, for it goes sorely against the grain,—"hate a conqueror more intensely than those of Herat the Afghan."

Our German friends seem to be unanimously of opinion that the treaty with the Ameer was an error of policy, and that if we withdrew within our own lines, busying ourselves with a frontier on the south instead of the north of Afghanistan, we should render India absolutely safe, while we should thereby relegate to the Russians a mission of subjugation and annexation in Central Asia, which would deprive them both of the wish and of the power to come into collision with their neighbours for a generation or two to come.

There is a letter from Lord Lawrence to Lord Canning under date, Kohat, Nov. 26, 1856, of which every elector

in the United Kingdom ought to have a copy. He says: "I have thought over this question to the best of my ability frequently and anxiously. I have read up all the information which I could procure, and have discussed the subject with some of the best officers in the army at different times; and the conclusion which has been invariably forced on my judgment, is, that it would be a fatal error for us to interfere actively in Central Asia. . . . I cannot perceive any reason why Russia could not throw into Herat any number of engineers and artillerymen she might think proper, long before our army could sit down in front of it. And these officers, with the assistance which Persia could supply in labour, would render it impregnable against all the means which we could bring from India against it. It is my conviction that any such attempt by us would not only entail the expenditure of millions, but would assuredly end in disaster. I admit that the interests of the Afghans are at present identical with ours, but it does not follow that such will always be the case. If we prove successful in the contest no doubt the Afghans will remain faithful. But in the event of a reverse it might prove their true game to take the other side. If we send an army to Afghanistan it must go prepared for all contingencies, to meet all comers, to depend solely on its own means and its own resources; and, at Herat, it would be many hundred

miles from our frontier, and from all effective support. . . . The Afghans are fickle and fanatical to a proverb, and their rulers have but a nominal control over them. Even if willing the latter could not ensure supplies, and the visits of the commissariat agents and contractors would soon prove eminently distasteful. I am equally averse to the minor or less dangerous measure of despatching an irregular force to garrison Candahar. If the Ameer cannot fight his own battles on his own ground, it seems vain for us to attempt to do it. The Persians may succeed in occupying Candahar for a time, but the possession will probably entail future disaster. The Afghans, if they ever can be induced to combine, will do so to get rid of such an invader. There can be no doubt that the Afghans, despite the natural strength of their country, and the martial character of the population, are really weak, owing to internecine quarrels, and the fickle and faithless character of the people. . . . If we send a force to Candahar it will eventually necessitate the re-occupation of the country. Afghanistan will then become the battle-field for India, and the cost of maintaining our position will render India bankrupt; and should we meet with reverses we shall have to retrace our steps, with an exhausted treasury and a dispirited army. Whereas, on the other hand, if we leave Afghanistan alone, and concentrate our means on this side of the

Suliman range, we should meet an invader worn by toil and travel, with a weak artillery, and distant from his resources, as he debouched from the passes. Under such circumstances defeat should be certain, and defeat would be annihilation. The money which we should expend in besieging Herat and in fighting in Afghanistan would double our European force in India, finish our most important railroads, and cover the Punjab river with steamers. I believe that the Cabul war from first to last did not consume less than twelve millions of money; and this is but a trifle compared to the sacrifices which would be necessary against Russia and Persia combined if we met them in Central Asia."

CHAPTER VII.

CONCLUSION OF THE WHOLE MATTER.

IT is melancholy to think how near we have been to war on account of incidents which concern, only in the remotest manner possible, the people of this country, and how little the facts of the case, the geography of the disputed territories, and the true interests of the two great countries most intimately concerned, are known and understood. Nature has clearly laid down the line beyond which (northward) it would be both impolitic and dangerous for us to go, and recent events have only too conclusively proved what a mistake it is to link our fortunes with those of semi-civilized races, and to penetrate into regions where we really have no business at all. There may be reasons why, in consequence of treaty engagements, some sort of temporary arrangement may not be altogether unadvisable; but the sooner a lasting one is made the better, and not until we are quit of all entangling alliances, and responsible only for our own doings, and not those of changeable and restless neigh-

bours, can we expect to get rid of these constant rumours of impending strife.

The arguments of Lord Lawrence seem irresistible. No one has, as yet, ventured, with any degree of success, to assail his position; and what the electors of the United Kingdom ought to insist on is, that the military advisers of the Governor-General of India, the Secretaries of State, and the British Cabinet, should fix upon and render impregnable a defensive frontier between our possessions and Afghanistan, which would render us indifferent to the proceedings of Russia, and deliver us from the increasing cost of vast and continually-recurring preparations for the defence of our Indian Empire.

CHAPTER VIII.

THE BEARING OF THE FOREGOING ON THE FEELING AND THE FINANCES OF INDIA—A PROVISO AND A CAUTION.

It must, however, be kept in mind that in thus constructing and rendering impregnable a natural frontier there must be no panic or haste, no attempt to divert, for defences in the North-west, anything like the whole of the sums that would otherwise have been expended in developing the resources of the country as a whole. Greatly to add to taxation, and at the same time to stop expenditure on railways, canals, and other works in India, would be to avoid one danger by incurring a much more serious one—and it looks, at present, as if we were about to commit this deplorable blunder.

It may, therefore, not be amiss briefly to pass in review our position in, and relations to our great dependency, which ought to be kept steadily in sight in all arrangements which are made regarding a scientific boundary.

A few years ago a British officer, who had been thirty-five years in the country, and thought that he knew all about the question, wrote: "Were India invaded

by a Russian or French army, the flame of insurrection would burst forth from Peshawur to Cape Comorin."

Let us hope that he has lived to learn how completely his predictions have been falsified by the event. The inhabitants of India no doubt do not particularly love us; there is, in fact, nothing that could be called political sentiment among the masses, their general attitude being one of indifference. "Phoo," said an old man to a planter in Mysore, "Rajah here, Queen there; whoever comes we must grind corn." Another remarked, "What can our rulers matter as long as we are let alone?" The educated portion of the community, however, know well, and the sentiment pervades every class and race, that our sway is better for them in every respect than that of Russia; and it was that certain knowledge which chiefly caused the remarkable outburst of loyalty towards the British crown, which lately astonished the world and stunned the war party in St. Petersburg.

Another, and perhaps a more powerful reason, was the noble policy of Lord Ripon, his Christian-like treatment of the natives, his refusal to be guided by cliques, his endeavours to extend the principle of local self-government, his protection of the weak against the strong, and all those courageous words and deeds, which natives of influence in every part of the land told the writer of these pages, had made him universally "beloved." His

English enemies are the evil counsellors who have so often endangered our Asiatic dominions, and their creed is perhaps summed up in a sentence which may be found in a book by one of them, who in his magnificent folly exclaimed, "Not India for the Indians, but India for Imperial Britain, say I!"

The Marquis of Ripon, and his administrative supporters, have laid us under a debt of gratitude, the value of which will never be known to the present generation. The attitude of the princes and people of India in the early part of this year, when external danger was apprehended, is a triumph greater than any ever awarded to Roman conqueror, a monument more enduring than brass.

In his famous speech in the House of Commons on December 1, 1783, on the question of going into committee on the first of Mr. Fox's East India Bills, Edmund Burke said:

"Our conquest there, after twenty years, is as crude as it was the first day. The natives scarcely know what it is to see the grey head of an Englishman. Young men (boys almost) govern there without society and without sympathy with the native. They have no more social habits with the people than if they still resided in England; nor, indeed, any species of intercourse but that which is necessary to making a sudden fortune with a view to a remote settlement. Animated with all the

avarice of age, and all the impetuosity of youth, they roll in one after another, wave after wave; and there is nothing before the eyes of the natives but an endless, hopeless prospect of new flights of birds of prey and passage, with appetites continually renewing for a food that is continually wasting. Every rupee of profit made by an Englishman is lost for ever to India. With us are no retributory superstitions by which a foundation of charity compensates, through ages to the poor, for the rapine and injustice of a day. With us no pride erects stately monuments which repair the mischiefs which pride had produced, and which adorn a country out of its own spoils. England has erected no churches, no hospitals, no palaces, no schools; England has built no bridges, made no high-roads, cut no navigations, dug out no reservoirs. Every other conqueror of every other description has left some monument, either of state or beneficence, behind him. Were we to be driven out of India this day, nothing would remain to tell that it had been possessed during the inglorious period of our dominion by anything better than the ourang-outang or the tiger."

The natives are quite aware of the general truth of this indictment, and no one who has travelled through the country can fail to be reminded in various ways of the poverty of the people; but substantial endeavours

are now being made to atone for our past neglect, and all recognize the fact which may be stated in Bishop Wilson's words, "Britain is the first conqueror which has blessed the whole of Hindostan with peace, and which has established a firm and righteous sovereignty."

Mr. Ferrier writes: " The superiority of the English policy and arms in India, has insured them their colossal dominions; and whatever may be said in Europe, their firmly seated power is less odious than that of the tyrants they have dispossessed." Elsewhere the writer has remarked, "Thousands of the upper classes among the natives are fast making money under our *régime* of law and order."[1]

Colonel Meadows Taylor says, "The people would not invest their capital unless the country were to remain under British rule, and I could not conscientiously counsel them to do so."

The editor of that excellent man's biography remarks : " Meadows Taylor gave to the people of India not only his head, but his heart. He had the liveliest sympathy and affection for the natives of India. Thoroughly understanding their traditions and their manners, he treated men and women of all ranks with the consideration and respect due to an ancient society."

And the colonel himself, towards the close of the

[1] "A Winter in India."

story of his life, expresses himself thus: "One word, one last reflection in regard to India, may not be out of place. It is to advise all who go there, in whatever capacity or whatever position they may hold: Use true courtesy to natives of all degrees. My experience has taught me that large masses of men are more easily led than driven, and that courtesy and kindness and firmness will gain many a point which under a hard and haughty bearing would prove unattainable."

In his valuable work, "India in 1880," Sir Richard Temple, late Governor of Bombay and Finance Minister of India, says: "The native character, as a whole, may be disparaged by some whose experience is short and whose knowledge is not profound. But with an Englishman who lives and labours in the country, the wider his acquaintance with the natives and the deeper his insight, the greater is his liking for them. He who has the best and longest acquaintance with the natives esteems them the most."

Formerly, impartial travellers of other nations remarked the "undisguised contempt" with which the English in India treated the natives, and the "impassable barrier" which existed between them. But a great change for the better has recently taken place, and the present generation, according to universal testimony, has greatly improved upon the manners and conduct of the past.

This danger to our continued sway in India is happily in course of being removed; it may be well to devote a few sentences to another. "Light taxation, in my mind," wrote Sir John Lawrence in 1866, "is the panacea for foreign rule in India;" and depend upon it, as education increases among the natives, we shall find more and more, as Sir Richard Temple puts it, that "Financial considerations really form the basis of that fabric upon which the Indian Empire rests."

Of two things we must emphatically beware, namely, of taxation for Imperial purposes, which would be felt to be unjust and oppressive by the natives, and of unfair exemptions in favour either of the native aristocracy or of Europeans.

"On the very last occasion on which I saw Lord Lawrence," says General Strachey, "he spoke to me to this effect: 'Temptations are never wanting in India for Government to earn for themselves an easy and apparent popularity by a refusal to impose taxes on the richer and more influential classes of the community; and while these, the only audible critics, approve, it will never be difficult to find acceptable means for a course essentially impolitic and unjust. Statesmen should never forget that the real foundations of our power in India do not rest on the interested approval of the noisy few. They rest on justice, on the contentment of the

millions who may not always be silent and quiescent, and on their feeling that, in spite of the selfish clamour of those who profess to be their guardians and representatives, they may place implicit trust in the equal justice of our Government, and in its watchful care of the interests of the masses of the people. The exemption of the richer classes from taxation is a political mistake, which, as time goes on, and knowledge and intelligence increase, must become more and more mischievous.'"

Such are the considerations which ought to guide our Government in all its dealing with the Indian people; and as long as we rule on these lines small attention need be paid to hostile demonstrations from abroad. Long ago Sir John Lawrence wrote from the Punjaub, "Our danger in India has been proved to come much more from within than from without."

The dangerous people in reality are, not the native warriors or the Russians, but the annexationists, the men who are never content with present boundaries, the men who advocated two wicked and disastrous campaigns in Afghanistan, the "dashing soldiers" and "adventurous politicians" who have expended, worse than uselessly, millions of money, and sacrificed thousands of lives, "without," as Mr. Bosworth Smith expresses it, "stopping the march of Russia by a single day."

. "The natives of India," says Sir Richard Temple, " as

a rule raise their voice decidedly for peace, not at any price, but at some sacrifice, rather than for incurring the risks of war, with the certainty of special taxation in the present, and the probability of the public burdens being augmented in the future. They certainly are adverse to an aggressive, and favourable to a pacific, policy."

By all means strengthen and render insurmountable a barrier on the North-west, but do so calmly and gradually, not in hot haste as if an enemy were at the doors. Take care, moreover, both in respect to it and in the general policy of the Government, not to over-tax the masses of the Indian people; and not to forget that they desire peace and quietness, and have no sympathy with that class of politicians who are never at rest, but are constantly looking around for signs and occasions of war.

CHAPTER IX.

THE RESPONSIBILITY OF WAR—BRITISH PUGNACITY—
THE STANDING ARMIES OF EUROPE A MENACE AND
DANGER—ARBITRATION A BETTER WAY.

"INCLINED as I am," said General Gordon, "with only a small degree of admiration for military exploits, I esteem it a far greater honour to promote peace than to gain any paltry honours in a wretched war." It is narrated of the Crown Prince of Germany that during his Bohemian campaign, on reaching elevated ground, and seeing all around him the signs of victory, he exclaimed with emotion to one of his staff, pointing to the field of blood, "What a responsibility is incurred by those who are the cause of war!"

A lamentably large portion of the political rulers, the courtiers, and the press of Europe, seems to treat this responsibility as a very light thing indeed. Generals and journalists in St. Petersburg and Moscow, think of promotion and decorations and pay, while Jingoes in London speak glibly and heartlessly of "a brush with

the Russians," as if it were a horse-race or a game at cricket. The waste of millions of money, and the sacrifice of thousands of brave men, are too little thought of by them in comparison with active employment, military glory, and the humiliation of a natural enemy. It makes one melancholy to observe how little progress has, after all, been made in substituting a better mode of settling differences.

Buckle says, "Every great increase in the activity of the human intellect has struck a blow at the warlike spirit."

And another great thinker, Horace Bushnell, in his essay on the "Growth of Law," thus puts it: "It is impossible that wars should not be discontinued, if not by the progress of the international code, as we have hinted, yet by the progress of liberty and intelligence; for the masses who have hitherto composed the soldiery must sometime discover the folly of dying, as an ignoble herd, to serve the passions of a few reckless politicians, or to give a name for prowess to leaders whose bravery consists in marching *them* into danger. The arbitrament of arms is not a whit less absurd than the old English trial-by-battle, and before the world has done rolling they will both be classed together."

Two sentences of Leigh Hunt's on this subject are

worth transcribing. "I now look upon war as one of the fleeting necessities of things in the course of human progress; as an evil (like most evils) to be regarded in relation to some other evil that would have been worse without it, but always to be considered as an indication of comparative barbarism; as a necessity, the perpetuity of which is not to be assumed, or as a half-reasoning mode of adjustment, whether of disputes or of populations, which mankind, on arriving at years of discretion, and coming to a better understanding with one another, may, and must of necessity, do away. It would be as ridiculous to associate the idea of war with an earth covered with railroads and commerce as a fight between Holborn and the Strand, or between people met in a drawing-room."

It would be difficult to find calm, dispassionate, and philosophic minds ready to dispute the position assumed by these writers; nor, indeed, would an antagonistic position be in accordance with common sense, to say nothing of Christianity. Yet how small a way have the so-called civilized nations gone on this path of enlightenment and peace! It is true that the Alabama arbitration produced a profound effect, and that the feeling between Great Britain and the United States has since wonderfully changed for the better. It is also true that other feebler attempts in the same direction have been made, but they

are treated with derision by powerful politicians and military men, and we seem very little nearer to the goal of settling international disputes, otherwise than by the coarse and barbarous resort to arms.

In this country there is nothing easier than to stir up the feelings of all classes in favour of aggressive measures. Justice, reason, and consistency, are alike thrown to the winds, when the English imagine that any one wishes to tread upon their toes. They want no further information; they brush aside the counsels of calmer advisers, and enthusiastically go in for fighting, to prove their dauntless spirit and their superiority over any of the other nations of the world.

How many unjust wars have they thus begun, "ringing the bells" to begin with, as Sir Robert Walpole wittily said, "but in the end wringing their hands." Cardinal de Retz remarked "that people are more frequently the dupes of suspicion than of confidence." This is conspicuously true of the British nation in its dealings with other Powers. There are politicians and newspapers whose speeches and articles you may read from year's end to year's end, without finding a single word in favour of France, Germany, Russia, or the United States. Their maxim is, "no doubt we are the people, and wisdom shall die with us," and this foolish assumption of universal superiority has, in past times, cost us a frightful

waste of blood and treasure. No other country can move a step in any direction without exciting our suspicion and jealousy; and the severe lessons which we have received, as to the folly of our interference in the affairs of other nations, seem to have left us little, if at all, wiser than we were before.

The following from the "Life of Sir David Wedderburn" may be studied with profit: "We cannot be too much upon our guard against that class of politicians who believe that the strength and resources of the British Empire necessarily increase with its territorial extensions, and who regard all conquests or annexations of rival nations as affording just cause for alarm. They appear to think that every barbarous country, and especially every island, all over the globe belongs, or ought to belong, to England. These 'patriots' are frantic with jealousy, lest another great Power should do *once* what England has done over and over again, and should attempt to share the British monopoly in civilizing aboriginals off the face of the earth. If other great nations are willing to undertake a share in the task of civilizing Africa or Asia, a far-sighted policy dictates ready acquiescence on our part, in what is really the imposition of a burden on the shoulders of a possible rival. Experience has taught us, in many wars, that remote colonies and

possessions are a serious encumbrance to a belligerent of inferior maritime force ; and in particular it has been proved again and again, that all islands occupied by the rivals of Great Britain are simply hostages placed in the hands of that Power which so long has ruled the seas. Not without reason is the British navy popular, giving, as it does, security at home and empire abroad, without menacing liberty or unduly burdening the exchequer.

"We possess already the most extensive empire that has ever existed on this globe, and a large proportion of this is still an unpeopled waste, requiring capital and labour to develop its splendid resources, and to support millions where now only thousands are found. There is an ample field for all our national energy within our existing borders, and the Englishman who advocates the wider extension of those borders far from the sea, our own element, into the heart of Africa or Asia, is no true friend to his country."

The curious thing, moreover, is that the advocates of this "Rule, Britannia" policy abroad, are the identical men who are the alarmists at home. Their grandfathers for a century believed that the possession—and, one would think, the very natural possession—of Dunkirk by France, was a source of imminent danger to England. Their fathers were angry with Nelson for ridiculing French invasion. The sons are never tired of calling

out for new forts, and more ships, and bigger guns, and great additions to the army, and God knows what, to protect us from men who are to cross the Channel in waterproof boots; from forces forty thousand strong, which are to be marshalled and transported in a manner, nobody knows how, so as to take Dover by a *coup de main*, and plunder London without any one being aware of their coming! No amount of military and naval expenditure satisfies these panic-mongers; if one half of their demands were granted, the nation would become bankrupt, and internal revolution would put a stop to external conquest.

There is a very instructive passage in Mr. Thorold Rogers's "Historical Gleanings": "Sir Robert Walpole had work to do in checking those influential people, who, as Lord Grantham did, with earnest patriotism and bad grammar, continually shouted out, 'I hate the French, and I hope as we shall beat the French.' That Walpole had a rational dislike for war, because he believed that it could always be avoided, and that its contingent advantages could never compensate for a tithe of the evils which it inevitably induces, is plain. He knew that a ministry which undertakes such a responsibility, however popular it is at first, is sooner or later unpopular; sooner, if the war policy be undertaken by error of judgment; later, even if the war be justified by the vulgar arts of demagogism."

It is now six and thirty years ago since Mr. Cobden said at Leeds: "It is not always necessary to hold up a scarecrow to frighten your neighbours. I believe a civilized nation will estimate the power of a country, not by the amount laid out in armaments, which may be the means of weakening that power, but it will measure your strength by your latent resources, what margin of taxation you have that you can impose in case of necessity, greater than another country to which you may be opposed; what is the spirit of your people, as having confidence in the institutions or government under which they live; what is the general intelligence of the people; what is, in every respect, their situation and capacity to make an effort, in case an effort were required."

Mr. Cobden, however, in this respect as in others, was far in advance of popular opinion, and not until this "universal soldiership," which is "stabbing the heart" of Europe, has brought about a terrible and widespread catastrophe, are the nations likely to learn how unutterable is their folly. At present Germany, Russia, France, Austria, and Italy have peace establishments aggregating more than two millions of men, taken away from industrial pursuits during the flower of their age, and thus inflicting a direct and indirect loss on the community, the amount of which it would be difficult indeed to over-estimate.

The very existence and presence of these armed men are directly provocative of another war; and wars nowadays are terribly destructive. The late war between France and Germany cost the former alone 550,000 lives, and 370 millions sterling. The Russian official account admits a loss of 260,000 men during the Crimea war. Mr. Kinglake says that that war "brought to the grave full a million of workmen and soldiers."

In the year 1807-8, as a consequence of Napoleon's ambition, and of our endeavours to dictate to France and Europe generally, every seventh person in England was a pauper. Well might Southey in various poems declaim against "the hideous face of war."

Facts and figures and reason, as well as holier considerations, are, however, too often forgotten when the angry passions and pride of nations, as well as of men, are aroused. Thus every effort ought to be made by the advocates of peace and mutual good-will, to prevent the deplorable errors of our ancestors from being repeated, to recall the conscience of the people to the dread realities of war, and to bring about a frame of mind less defiant, suspicious, and jealous, and more impressed with a sense of deep responsibility as regards the sacrifice of human life—a feeling such as that described in the graphic words of the poet—

"Sick of the scene where War with ruthless hand
Spreads desolation o'er the bleeding land ;
Sick of the tumult, where the trumpet's breath
Bids Ruin smile, and drowns the groan of Death."

If Great Britain and Russia differed about a frontier in Asia—if they differ now—the whole matter, and not a mere incident in connection with it, should be submitted to arbitration. For two great nations, in consequence of such a dispute, to go to war on land and sea, involving miseries too terrible for tongue of man to tell, appears so foolish and criminal, so unreasonable and wicked, that it is hard on retrospect to believe that the deed of darkness was very nearly done.

The new electors should place and keep questions of this kind in the forefront of the battle. Candidates may use big words about economy, but if, in the inevitable international disputes of the future, war is to be the sole tribunal, they will prove mere hollow phrases, useful only to deceive.

APPENDICES.

APPENDICES.

No I.

FROM THE REVIEW OF THE MONTH IN "MACMILLAN'S MAGAZINE" FOR JUNE, 1885.

"On the last Monday of last month the Prime Minister electrified the House of Commons by a speech which was understood to point to a war with Russia. The stroke was sudden. Men were not prepared for so rapid an evolution of the crisis. The public were surprised, and a little bewildered. On the Saturday evening of the same week the usual brilliant circle of eminent guests were gathered together at the annual banquet of the Royal Academy. Under the glitter of the scene was felt the presence of grave preoccupations. It was known that Ministers had been hastily summoned during the afternoon to a Council for the consideration of the decisive reply from Russia. They were the last to arrive; but before men had all found their places at table, the rumour ran half secretly round the hall that the Russian answer had been a compliance, that reasonable terms were within reach, and that there was good assurance of peace. Later in the evening the Foreign Secretary gave authority to the whisper.

"If the affairs of an empire could be carried on by the

arts that make the after-dinner speaker, Lord Granville would have been a statesman of the first force. The most felicitous speech that he ever made cannot have produced a better effect than the not very felicitous sentence of May 2, in which he declared to the princes, ambassadors, soldiers, and all the rest of the illustrious world before him, his confident belief that nothing would happen to prevent men from continuing works of peace.

"On the following Monday Mr. Gladstone confirmed these good hopes by a specific declaration that Russia had come to an agreement, or was ready to do so, upon the following points. She was willing to submit to the judgment of the sovereign of a friendly State the question whether the movements of Komaroff were consistent with the understanding of March 16 between the two Governments: that is to say, whether the understanding made it incumbent on the Russian Government to issue to Komaroff other instructions than those on which he took such remarkable action. That much being settled, there was no reason why the two Governments should not at once resume their communications in London as to the main points of the line for the delimitation of the Afghan frontier. When the main points were settled, then the officers of the two Governments would examine and trace the actual details of the line on the spot. This was on May 4. During the three weeks that have since elapsed, the clouds have slowly to some degree gathered again. It was not indeed to be expected that negotiations containing so many elements of detail should go on as if they were a transaction for the sale of a horse. The character of Russia is not good in the British political market. This makes the least delay a

source of suspicion and uneasiness. The papers that have been laid before Parliament neither raise the credit of St. Petersburg for sincerity, nor of London for knowingness and foresight. The action of the Czar in sending a sword of honour to General Komaroff created a profound and most justifiable irritation. We do not expect a fine and chivalrous taste in the hard transaction of rough business; it may be that the Czar sent Komaroff his sword to console the military party for seeing submitted to arbitration the question whether the Czar had not broken an agreement in ordering Komaroff to undertake the exploit for which he decorated him. This may be. It only shows that on one side, at any rate, the conditions of peace still depend on the simple ethics of a Cossack camp. In all this unpleasant proceeding we are only reaping what we have sown, and undergoing the mortifications incident to a position that was not taken up with full consideration and well-devised preparation.

"When these difficulties are all settled, it is obvious that, on the theory of the buffer-State, a more serious and enduring one would remain. Nobody can disguise from himself that when the Afghan frontier is fixed, the Russians will only feel bound to respect it on condition that we make the Afghans respect it. As the Duke of Argyll put this point (May 12), the question of paramount importance is whether, in the absence of complete control over Afghanistan, we are to be practically responsible for their border-quarrels, of which there will be perpetual danger, and which it will be extremely hard to restrain. Opinion moves, for the most part, in one way as to the true policy in view of liabilities of this description. Lord Salisbury said—

"'I hope we shall do all we can to conciliate and keep the Ameer of Afghanistan with us, and to help him to the utmost of our power to defend his country. But do not let the desire of his friendship lead us into either of those two mistakes—either in making ourselves responsible for any of the excesses which the wild tribes under his control may commit upon his western frontier; nor, on the other hand, can we make any susceptibilities which any Afghan ruler may feel a reason for abstaining from defending, and defending adequately, those positions we may consider absolutely necessary for the strength of our own position.'

" From the last, as a general proposition, there can be little dissent, though of course there is room for ample difference of opinion, whether military or political, as to the points at which this absolute necessity would begin. On both sides it was agreed, in the course of the debate in the House of Lords, that Herat is not a very promising scene of British operations. Lord Salisbury is of the same opinion as Lord Kimberley, that 'the prospect of defending Herat by British troops is not one which seems to the non-military mind very attractive or very feasible. It may always be possible for us, with assistance in the shape of arms and officers, to assist the Ameer in defending that place, but to defend it ourselves, I confess, seems to me a dangerous undertaking.' The Secretary for India had said, with his well-known emphasis, that 'the schemes which are put forward to the effect that we should create and make Herat a great Indian or British fortress, to be held by British and Indian troops at a great distance from our frontier, and among a population not under our direct influence, would involve us in great and serious dangers.' But,

then, Lord Kimberley went on to say that this would 'not prevent us from doing what may be done to strengthen the Ameer's position at Herat, and to put the fortifications there in a condition to afford a reasonable amount of security. That is a different thing from making Herat an English frontier fortress.' The difference is hardly so plain as we could wish, though we may admit that the two British officers who are now actually in Herat with the full consent of Abdur Rahman may be there in virtue of our obligations to that prince. But, if our policy is to be consistent, the time is sure to come when these obligations will have to be revised. Supposing that, for reasons which it is easy to imagine, from hard roubles down to *force majeure*, an Afghan Ameer were to let the Russians into Herat, it would, in Lord Salisbury's judgment, which most sensible men will not dispute, be 'a dangerous undertaking' for us either to turn them out or to prevent them from coming in. We have to face this contingency—of an unfriendly or pro-Russian Ameer. What then would be the policy?

"Lord Kimberley has given us the answer. 'In that case,' he said, ' our defence would have to be based on a strictly defensive system within our own lines. One thing is certain—that we ought not to found our policy on the notion that we should construct a frontier line in Central Asia, for which this country would be entirely responsible, several hundreds of miles distant from our base.' Here, again, there followed the perilous qualification, arising from the present arrangement: 'Of course by an alliance with the Afghans we must undertake a considerable responsibility for that frontier; and we hope that a satisfactory frontier line will be drawn between Russian and Afghan territory. That would render it

necessary that some of our officers should be present on that frontier.' That is to say, the present alliance plants us in a position from which a change in the Ameer's way of thinking might make it indispensable that we should retreat, yet from which we could certainly not retreat without giving colour to the imputation that we had been worsted and driven back by Russia. Here is the element of danger in the half-policy, or the two-faced and ambiguous policy, to which we are now temporarily committed.

"The policy of to-day, we say, can only be temporary. The zone and the buffer have had their day. However the settlement of the Afghan frontier may fall out, it is agreed that 'it is impossible for us any longer to have the satisfaction of knowing that we are in an insular position in India.' We may not have exactly reached the stage, so long anticipated by Cobden and others, when India and Russia are conterminous, but we are within a measurable distance of such a stage. The Government is framing new propositions in accordance with a new state of things. A project of frontier defence has been approved, and authority has been given for the expenditure of a sum of £5,000,000 on frontier railways and military roads, including the Quetta railway, which will cost something like £2,000,000 of that sum. Five millions are not supposed to be the final limit, but so much will at least be required for the railway and the military road. It is pretty certain to be found on further examination that further works will have to be undertaken. Lord Dufferin thinks it is a matter for serious consideration whether there should not be strong fortresses on the same line to give our army support. Peshawur, the Indus, and Quetta mark the general

direction and the limits of the line. More detailed particulars were laid before the House of Commons by the Indian Under-Secretary, who (May 21) added the information that of the five millions required, a part would fall upon the revenues of India, and a part would be met by a loan to be issued by the Secretary of State with the sanction of Parliament. All this indicates an immense transformation in the position of the Indian Empire. The consequences may be more far-reaching than to careless observers may at first sight appear. The key to internal security in India is thrift. Heavy expenditure means heavy taxation, and that means discontent. The cost of the new frontier must bring with it an augmentation of burdens, as well as the diversion to military defence of funds that might more fruitfully have gone, under a happier star, to the development of the productive resources of the country."

No. II.

On October 1, 1842, *Lord Ellenborough* wrote as follows:

"The Government of India, content with the limits nature appeared to have assigned to its empire, would henceforth devote all its efforts to the establishment and maintenance of general peace, to the protection of the sovereigns and chiefs, its allies, and to the happiness and prosperity of its own faithful subjects; that the rivers of the Punjab and the Indus, and the mountainous passes and the barbarous tribes of Afghanistan, would be placed between the British army and an enemy approaching from the west, and no longer between the army and its supplies."

No. III.

On January 7, 1854, *Sir John Lawrence* wrote: "Should a Russo-Persian army invade Afghanistan, the invasion would unite the Afghans against them. Let us only be strong on this side the passes, and we may laugh at all that goes on in Kabul. I would waste neither men nor money beyond."

On January 30, 1857, *Sir John Lawrence* wrote: " The effect of the possession of Herat by an enemy on the minds of the natives of India must, of course, be a matter of opinion. I myself do not think that they will trouble themselves on the subject. I believe I know the natives and their opinions and feelings as well as most British officers, and I was at Delhi, the seat of the Mohammedan population, during the first siege of Herat in 1839, and, neither then nor in the present instance have I perceived that the natives felt much interest in the subject. One of the arguments for the advance into Afghanistan in 1839-40 was that a general feeling of excitement, a general feeling adverse to our rule, existed in Upper India. I never myself saw a symptom of it; and the best evidence that such was not the case is that, even after unprecedented disasters, no such feeling was shown. I believe that there is no man now alive who will ever see a Russian army in India, and no Asiatic army could stand for a day before our troops in the open plain. To do anything against us in the field, a large body of good

European troops with plenty of artillery, and the whole in proper order, must come. A large army cannot come rapidly through the intervening countries even between the Oxus and the Indus without being demoralized; and if a small force should advance, or a large force attempt it by slow degrees — in one case they will be beaten, and in the other they will not be able to feed themselves. Afghanistan does not grow food for a large army of strangers. It can scarcely feed its own population. No means of transport exist for such a force. Carts, there are none, nor roads along which they could move."

Seven years later he said: "Make India, as it is in your power to do, peaceful, prosperous, and contented first. Assure the neighbouring tribes that you do not covet their territory and will not meddle with their independence, and then *when* Russia comes—if ever she does come—with hostile intention, they will be to you as a wall of adamant against her."

No. IV.

OPINION OF SIR RICHARD TEMPLE.

"India in 1880"—*p.* 423.

"For many years past, notably since 1857, when Russia began to operate against Bokhara, and still more since she subjugated Khiva, there have been apprehensions aroused in India. The alarm felt in Afghanistan on account of the Russian operations in Khiva communicated itself to many Indian authorities; and these apprehensions have assumed different shapes. Some persons feared that the proceedings of Russia were tending solely to one purpose, namely, the invasion of India. The plundering of this fertile and populous country was to be offered to the Afghans as a bait for inducing them to join the invaders. These extreme views have been dissipated by considerations relating to Russia itself. She has too many distractions at home to prevent her from engaging in complications abroad. Her power of aggression has been proved by experience to be less than might be supposed from the strength of her army, and her financial resources are restricted. Her position in Central Asia is not, as yet, sufficiently consolidated to serve as a base for operating against a foreign power. If she attempted to establish herself in Afghanistan, she would encounter the very difficulties of which England has had such bitter experience."

No. V.

Russia in Poland.

"Russia has been justly blamed for the severities which she inflicted on Poland. In judging of the relations of the two countries it should, however, be remembered—first, that for six centuries there had been continual war between Poland and Russia; that Poland was habitually the aggressor; that, being then the stronger, she inflicted terrible evils upon Russia, and sought by diplomacy, as well as by war, to strangle the national life of her rival. When Russia, now grown strong, shared in the final assault upon Poland, she was not attacking a harmless neighbour, she was avenging centuries of cruel wrong. Second, at the time of the dismemberment the Poles were in the lowest state of degradation, ignorant, indolent, poor, drunken, and improvident." The recent reports of the English consuls represent the condition of Poland as most satisfactory. There is "a very remarkable progress in commerce, agriculture, and manufactures." "The country is becoming rich and prosperous beyond all expectation" (*Mackenzie's* "The Nineteenth Century," pp. 349, 379).

No. VI.

FROM "THE WESTMINSTER REVIEW," OCT., 1867.

"The balance of opinion is fortunately over-riding the ridiculous fears of Anglo-Indians at the progress of Russians towards Bokhara. If this satrapy were annexed to the Czar's dominions to-morrow, the only effect would be to put a stop to an iniquitous traffic in white slaves, as has been pointed out by Vambéry in the first instance, and since by M. Guillaume Lejean, in an article in the *Revue de Deux Mondes*. The remarks of this latter gentleman, directed as they are against the prevailing opinion of his countrymen, which are anti-Russian, are well worth attentive study; and if we take the abolition of the slave traffic carried on by the Turkomans alone into consideration, it is rather hard to explain on what grounds we would limit the emancipation of humanity. Is it perfectly consistent to praise the emancipation of serfs, and cry aloud if he attempts to touch the chains of the Eastern serfs? No! Such civilization as the Russian people yet possess may with advantage be carried into the vast regions of Central Asia, until, touching the same Himalayan range, English and Russian shall rejoice together that they have replaced effete races, and swept away the barbarity of the Emirs who ruled them."

FROM "THE WESTMINSTER REVIEW," JULY, 1885.

"In this condition of things lies the weakness of Russia. It is evident that any country in such a state is on the verge of a change which may take either the form

of a peaceful reform, or of a revolutionary convulsion; and the longer it is delayed the more likely it is to take the more violent form. No such country can be really a dangerous foe in war. If the attention of the Government and its resources in men and money be absorbed in a foreign war, the better is the opportunity for Russian Liberals at home to rise against them. . . . Stepniak's estimate of his countrymen's peaceful disposition corroborates what Mr. Cobden said of them: 'The Russians are, perhaps, naturally the least warlike people in the world. All their tastes and propensities are of an opposite character. Even in their amusements there is an absence of rudeness and violence.' And he supports his opinion by that of one whose views on the Eastern Question did not generally agree with his own, Mr. Danby Seymour, who, in his volume on ' Russia and the Black Sea,' remarks, 'The most singular thing is that the people among whom this military organization of the whole nation prevails is, without exception, the most pacific nation on the face of the earth, and upon this point, I believe, no difference of opinion exists among all observers.'"

No. VII.

OPINION OF MAJOR-GENERAL SIR HENRY RODES GREEN, K.C.S.I., FROM HIS ARTICLE, "THE 'GREAT WALL' OF INDIA," IN "THE NINETEENTH CENTURY" FOR MAY, 1885.

"It would be of great advantage to England if at the present moment the idea could be removed from the minds of the English people that Herat is in any way the key of India. Some thirty years ago, very many of those who were then considered to be experts on Central Asian politics believed it to be so, but in later years a better knowledge of its real position and value has been gained, and it is now known that if an invasion of India is ever contemplated by a foreign power, there are other and better roads leading towards the Indian frontier than that *viâ* Herat; nevertheless for many reasons it would be a valuable acquisition, and that Russia will occupy this position at some no very distant date, there can I think be little doubt; and the almost certainty of her doing so will, I hope, compel the people of England to turn their serious attention to the strengthening of the natural frontier of India, which has already been commenced, and which may be made, I believe, absolutely impregnable.

"I trust, therefore, that all efforts will now be concentrated on this object, and that wild and impracticable schemes for attempting to turn Russia out of Herat, or of taking possession of it ourselves, will be put on one

side for ever; such schemes can only lead to enormous expenditure both of treasure and life, and to no practical results.

"Let us examine our present Indian frontier, which commences to the south, on the Indian Ocean near the seaport of Kurrachee, and ends on the north at Peshawer. Along this whole length, a distance of some 750 miles, runs the Suliman range of mountains, varying in height and ruggedness and pierced by many passes, the two main ones being the Bolan and the Kyber, and joining the Himalayan ranges north of Peshawer. To the east, along the foot of these mountains, nearly for their whole length, runs a strip of desert, then comes a fringe of cultivation, then the river Indus, unfordable at any point from its mouths to beyond Peshawer, which it passes at Attock—to the west of this range, marking the Indian frontier, between the Kyber and the Bolan passes, lies Afghanistan, with which country and the character of its inhabitants we are already too well acquainted, and we may here call to mind the remark of the Great Duke of Wellington, that it was a country in which 'a small army would be annihilated, and a large one starved.'

"I may here mention that there had never been any question of occupying any point whatever in Afghanistan. It was not until 1876 that the Government of India began to think that the ideas of General Jacob and his successor were not 'visionary anticipations,' and Quettah was occupied, and now represents what General Jacob called the 'bastion of the front attacked,' and which should be made by our engineer officers as strong and secure from attack as science can effect. Running south from Quettah, of which it forms a part, is the plateau of Beloochistan, varying in elevation for a distance of 200

miles from Quettah to Kozdar, of from 4,000 to 6,800 feet above the sea level, and connected with British territory by comparatively easy passes in friendly hands; along this plateau we might locate our European soldiers, in a salubrious climate, ready at a very short notice to concentrate at Quettah, which station would be by rail within forty-eight hours of the seaport of Kurrachee, and within three weeks from London itself. This position would constitute our left flank defence, as no army of any serious dimensions could march towards India through the deserts of Mekran lying west of Beloochistan and extending to the Indian Ocean. We should now have to provide for the defence of the remaining 400 miles of the Punjaub frontier between Mithencote and Peshawer, running along the foot of the Suliman range of mountains. On this line we ought, I think, to construct strong defensive works to command the debouchures of the numerous passes. Mithencote, Dehra Gazee Khan, Dehra Ishmael Khan, Bunnoo, Kohat, and Peshawer, the latter commanding the exits from the Kyber Pass, would probably be some of the points selected; behind this line we have the Indus river, nowhere fordable, and which in summer is very broad and rapid—in some parts during that season it has a width of from four to five miles. This splendid river might be patrolled by any number of iron gun and torpedo boats. Peshawer would form our right flank of defence; and here, in addition to a fortress, we might construct a strongly entrenched camp, and with the railroad which has already reached to this point we should have the vast resources of Northern India at our command to meet any army debouching from the Kyber, while from the other extremity at Quettah we could draw *via* Kurra-

chee on the resources not only of India, but from England direct; in fact, we should have close at our backs all the material and resources which England and India could supply, and in addition those of our colonies. Under such favourable circumstances, I think we have only to remain cool, husband our vast strength, and in case of war let Russia do her worst. Now let us analyse the position of that Empire supposing she possessed herself of Herat.

"We certainly hear much of the power of that valley to maintain and supply an army for aggressive operations, but can its means of doing so compare in any way with those at the disposal of India for defensive purposes, as I have endeavoured to point out? Even were Herat connected by rail direct with Russia itself, the power of supply would be very limited in comparison to that of England, with the assistance of our commercial marine, and our command of the sea. An attack on such a position as I have suggested we should hold on the frontier of India would require the concentration at Herat of at least 200,000 men and 600 guns, for the advance, the line of communication, and reserves, and in addition hundreds of thousands of baggage animals, exclusive of camp-followers.

"We must also consider the time that would be required for the concentration of such a force; it would then have to commence a march by Afghanistan, a distance of 500 miles through a poorly provided country, but having accomplished this, which would take some months—during which period I hope we should not be idle—in what condition would the Russian forces arrive on our border? And even supposing it possible for her to force a passage through the mountain ranges border-

ing our frontier, she would find the river swarming with all the latest inventions, in the shape of gun and torpedo boats, and an army on the opposite bank. I leave it to the imagination to picture what the feeding of such a vast host means in a country able only to sustain its own population. We will now suppose that Russia in course of time obtained full possession of Afghanistan, she would have a very poor country added to those which she already holds, and at the same time a most turbulent and expensive one to govern. We know that her possessions in Central Asia already cost her a cruel annual deficit in her treasury; the possession of Afghanistan would vastly increase it: she certainly would be conterminous with India, and we are warned that in such a position her intrigues might be dangerous to our existence as a governing power in that country; but is her form of government, or is it ever likely to be, so superior to ours as to lead the natives of India to wish for a change? I think not; but, on the contrary, from contemplating it from a nearer point, they would cling closer to us, and a mutual feeling of self-protection would still further strengthen the ties of sympathy which the present crisis has undoubtedly drawn forth from all classes of our Indian subjects, as well as from the independent princes both within and beyond our Indian Empire. Under such conditions, is Russia really to be feared as a close neighbour?"

No. VIII.

FROM "THE STATESMAN'S YEAR-BOOK," 1885.

In 1882 the Revenue of Russia was £70,371,150; the Expenditure £71,115,686.

"The finances of Russia exhibit large annual deficits." Since 1822 Foreign Loans have been raised amounting to £202,990,000; "several loans for railways guaranteed by the Imperial Government are not included in the above."

"On 1st January, 1884, the public debt of Russia amounted to £578,000,000, exclusive of the railway debt, but inclusive of a very large quantity of paper money with forced currency."

"The Russian Empire comprises one-seventh of the terrestrial part of the globe."

"The net receipts of Russian Railways in 1881 were 55,034,068 roubles, as against 75,960,075 roubles in 1878."

www.ingramcontent.com/pod-product-compliance
Lightning Source LLC
Chambersburg PA
CBHW031443160426
43195CB00010BB/834